Good Morning Rituals

DAILY RITUALS TO HELP YOU RISE AND SHINE

Miranda Moore

GOOD MORNING RITUALS

An Hachette UK Company
www.hachette.co.uk

Vie Books, an imprint of Summersdale Publishers Ltd
Part of Octopus Publishing Group Limited
Carmelite House
50 Victoria Embankment
LONDON
EC4Y 0DZ
UK

www.summersdale.com

Printed and bound in China

ISBN: 978-1-80007-926-7

Substantial discounts on bulk quantities of Summersdale books are available to corporations, professional associations and other organizations. For details contact general enquiries: telephone: +44 (0) 1243 771107 or email: enquiries@summersdale.com.

CONTENTS

Introduction

This little book is here to introduce you to a wonderful selection of morning rituals. These actions are designed to get your day off to a positive start and add value to your life – and they only take a few minutes of your time. With dozens of rituals to choose from, you can discover those that resonate with you, and then curate your own personal collection to help you feel calm, grounded and energized.

A ritual is an action that is performed with reverence and awareness. With repetition, these familiar sequences can take on a meditative quality, allowing you to begin your day with slow acceptance and gratitude. By starting your morning well, you are building a strong foundation to carry that feeling of calm purpose through your day. Over time, these habitual actions can promote a baseline of satisfaction and peace, leaving you feeling more in control. So goodbye, mindless rushing – and hello, mindful mornings!

The Art of Rituals

A daily habit of a few handpicked
rituals truly is an art. By developing
and practising morning rituals, you can
be calmer, clearer, and more at ease
with your life and your circumstances.
Taking the time and making the
commitment to do these rituals is an act
of mindful self-care in a hectic world.

WHAT ARE RITUALS?

Rituals are simple sequences of actions performed mindfully in a set pattern, with an attitude of respect and dignity. They only take a few minutes to perform and have a clear purpose or intention behind them. Choosing rituals that intuitively appeal to you or address some specific issue in your life will provide you with a strong mental base for tackling whatever crops up during your day. With long-term practice, these repetitive actions can help you to become better equipped to handle whatever life throws your way by building an underlying sense of calmness.

WHAT ARE
THE BENEFITS?

Specific benefits will vary, depending on what you are trying to achieve. You may notice improved well-being, lower stress levels or a more positive mindset. The familiarity of a repeated sequence allows you to pause and check in with yourself, and these actions can imbue you and your day with a sense of peace and purpose. For example, if you perform a ritual for gratitude, mental clarity or calm, your body and mind will recognize the actions and will be primed to respond accordingly – like a code or shortcut to a desired outcome.

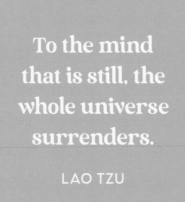

To the mind
that is still, the
whole universe
surrenders.

LAO TZU

WHY MAKE TIME FOR MORNING RITUALS?

If you sit on a street bench in the morning and observe your surroundings, you are likely to see people rushing all around you – our modern world is a relentlessly busy one. By ring-fencing a few minutes of precious time to commit to rituals, you can add energy, clarity and peace to your life. Engaging in an act of kindness to yourself also contributes to the world around you – because your sense of stability and calm will rub off on others, too. You can choose as many or as few as you like and tweak these rituals or create your own.

I ACCEPT THIS DAY AND ALL THAT IT BRINGS

My morning is already too busy!

If you think it will be impossible for you to find space in your morning for rituals, then you're exactly the sort of person who will benefit the most from introducing a few! If this sounds counterintuitive, consider that learning how to conduct your morning mindfully means you will be present in your life rather than existing on autopilot. Eating your breakfast mindfully may take no longer than eating it absent-mindedly, but the benefits will be greater.

Many rituals don't take long and are more about retraining your mind to pay attention than about adding extra tasks. For example, splashing your face with cold water can take seconds, repeating a mantra could be done silently on a train and writing in a gratitude journal might take two minutes, but all will quietly deliver rewards for the rest of the day. It's a qualitative question of how you spend your morning rather than any measure of time. However busy you are, a few rituals will help you to live each day more meaningfully.

TIME IS
A CREATED
THING. TO SAY
"I DON'T HAVE
TIME," IS LIKE
SAYING, "I DON'T
WANT TO."

LAO TZU

RITUALS
FOR SPECIFIC
OUTCOMES

Sometimes, you might turn to rituals to help
you deal with a difficult task or relationship,
or to calm you when you're faced with a
challenging situation. Research by behavioural
scientists at Harvard Business School
shows that rituals can help with self-control,
confidence, motivation, performance and
processing emotion. They can even be
effective in helping us cope with anxiety
and grief, since mentally processing an
action to address intense feelings helps us to
regain an element of control. You're training
your mind and body to take comfort in
the symbolic nature of the ritual, so you're
then fortified to continue with your day.

SYMBOLIC VALUE

Psychological studies show that rituals can have a positive impact on people's thoughts, feelings and behaviours. They are more than a mere sequence of activities. Since rituals signify moments of intention and importance, they are imbued with deeper meaning, beyond simple actions, helping us to navigate our life journey. Their value lies in what they represent for the person performing them. Committing to a ritual is respecting and safeguarding your inner peace in a busy world.

IT IS SO EASY TO
OVERESTIMATE
THE IMPORTANCE
OF ONE DEFINING
MOMENT AND
UNDERESTIMATE
THE VALUE OF
MAKING SMALL
IMPROVEMENTS
ON A DAILY BASIS.

JAMES CLEAR

Setting you up
for your day

Think of any top sports star and you are likely
to associate this person with some actions they
repeatedly perform at the beginning of every
match or competition. Similarly, many successful
actors and presenters perform distinctive rituals
before performing or speaking. The familiarity of
the action helps to calm their nerves, and signal
to their mind and body that they are prepared
for the task ahead. In the same way, you can
develop your own routine of rituals to set you up
for the day, empowering you to feel that you are
the driver in your life, rather than a bystander.

I AM WORTHY OF CONTENTMENT

ARE RITUALS FOR EVERYONE?

Rituals are for anyone and everyone – and can be performed anywhere, in whatever way suits your lifestyle and commitments. Your own practice is entirely personal to you, so your bespoke choice of rituals can be tailored to fit your schedule. Offering vital headspace, they can help anyone, from any profession or walk of life, to approach their day with clarity and focus. You can perform them while you get ready for your day, as you exercise or during your commute. Developing your own routine can give you a sense of calm and control – something beneficial to us all.

I HAVE EVERYTHING I NEED WITHIN MYSELF

PLEASURE IS ALWAYS DERIVED FROM SOMETHING OUTSIDE YOU, WHEREAS JOY ARISES FROM WITHIN.

ECKHART TOLLE

Rise and Shine

Immediately after waking is a great time to dive straight into your favourite rituals, thus beginning your day with familiarity and focus. Whether it's breathing exercises, yoga, stretches, meditation, a gratitude ritual, a glass of water or a couple of minutes outdoors, the options are limitless. Here are a few ideas to get you started.

TAKING STOCK

When you first wake up, before you climb
out of bed, take a few moments to take
stock and bring awareness to your body.
Notice your arms and legs, your torso,
chest, back, neck and head. How are you
feeling today? Observe sensations in your
body and any mood or emotion that you
perceive. If anything feels stifled, knotted
or uncomfortable, send it a little love and
compassion – visualize a small army of
friendly helpers flooding the area with
joyful energy. Allow your facial muscles to
relax, your eyebrows to soften and a gentle
smile to settle, and give thanks for this day.

GIVE
YOURSELF
TIME

To avoid feeling the physical and mental
stress that we encounter when we're
rushing, give yourself plenty of time in
the morning. An extra half-hour can
provide that necessary window of time
to make it feel like you can breathe, and
to make your morning a pleasant and
mindful part of your day. Plan when
you would like to get up, in order to
create space in your morning, and avoid
that feeling of being under pressure.

DIGITAL DETOX

It's a good idea to have a period in the morning before you turn on any screens or gadgets, unless you have personal reasons why you need to check a device. If you can, make the first half-hour or hour of your morning tech-free. This means your mind has a chance to warm up to the day and enjoy a vital window of calm before switching on a device. For example, if you have a few messages coming in as soon as you switch on your phone, your mind is immediately drawn into a task-oriented mode of thinking, and you can feel obligated to reply. Your mental and physical stress is likely to be higher than if you give yourself a few moments of self-care before you choose to check your devices.

Turning off notifications is also a simple step you can take, so that your phone isn't pinging throughout the morning with alerts, raising your stress and lowering your contentment.

You can live your whole life in one place and never really look at it.

LAUREN OLIVER

GLASS OF WATER

Drinking a glass of water after waking up is a great habit to develop, to rehydrate you following a night of sleep. Fill a glass with cold water and notice the way it swirls around. Sip the water, and feel it seep through your system, bringing essential hydration to every cell in your body. Notice how much nicer your mouth and throat feel. Your skin and other organs, too, will reap the benefits. Be grateful for this vital element that makes up roughly 60 per cent of your body and makes life possible.

TODAY, I CHOOSE KINDNESS

Gratitude ritual

Taking a couple of minutes every morning to reflect on what you're grateful for is an excellent way to cultivate positivity and notice all the good things in your life. In a journal, write down some things you're thankful for each day. It could be specific, like a snowflake, a sunrise or a bird singing; it could be a child's tiny hand in yours, a warm home or a particular friendship. It could be a wider concept, like peace, freedom or love. Reflect on each in turn, taking time to truly appreciate what they add to your life.

Raising your *qi*

This is a meditation technique from the ancient Chinese practice of *qigong* (pronounced *chee-gong*) and can be used to raise your energy. Ideally, perform it outside or looking out through a window.

Stand rooted on the floor, your feet planted hip-width apart. On an inhale, raise your arms to shoulder height in front of you, then lower them on your exhale. With each inhale, imagine you are pulling up energy from the universe and bringing it into your body. Allow your arms to feel light but strong. Continue to raise and lower your arms for a few minutes, focusing on your breath, the movement and your energy.

In traditional Chinese medicine, *qi* provides the energy for all your essential functions like metabolism, digestion, strength and mental focus. In this belief system, *qi* is the source of all life energy, and everything in the universe vibrates with it. Flowers are believed to possess concentrated *qi*, as the peak blossoming of the plant. By raising your *qi*, you are inviting and collecting this energy into your being.

Observe your breath

Paying attention to your breath is a simple skill that can be extraordinarily effective in helping you to deal with anxiety and calm a racing mind. Often, our minds can speed past the here and now, speculating on some possible future scenario or ruminating on a regret, to the point where we're missing the present moment of our lives. Coming back to your body and your breath means returning to the here and now. Simply observe your breath, as you inhale and exhale with focus. Notice it flowing in and out of your nostrils, replenishing you.

I RETURN TO MY BREATH; I RETURN TO THE HERE AND NOW

COMPASSION MEDITATION

A simple compassion meditation is an excellent
daily practice. Sit, allowing your breathing
to settle and your attention to centre.

With deep sincerity, repeat the words: "May I
be at ease; may I be free from suffering," until
you have settled into a hypnotic rhythm.

Now think of a person in your life. Really bring
this individual to mind, and feel their vulnerability
safe with you. Repeat the phrase: "May you be at
ease; may you be free from suffering," and truly
mean the words from the depth of your soul.
Send serenity, strength and freedom their way.

MEDITATION MEANS SIMPLE ACCEPTANCE.

YESHE LOSAL

MORNING SALUTATION

A simple stretch to salute the sun
simultaneously stretches your body
and relaxes the mind. Stand outside,
your feet hip-width apart and your
hands facing forwards by your sides.
Inhaling through your nose, slowly
raise your arms overhead, pulling them
backwards and squeezing your shoulder
blades together. Clasp your hands
above your head, reaching up through
your fingertips, and look up to the sky.
Breathing out, bring your hands down to
a prayer position in front of your chest.
Repeat twice, with a spirit of gratitude
to the life-giving power of the sun.

REMOVING
YOUR ARMOUR

Much of the time, people seem to be bracing themselves for some negative eventuality. This consumes a lot of our energy reserves, preparing for a battle that isn't present.

Imagine you are wearing a suit of heavy armour. You don't need it, because you are strong, not vulnerable. Piece by piece, mentally remove your armour, physically acting this out and laying each piece on the floor. Now you can feel lighter and looser. Shake your body and breathe in, filling yourself with vitality. This is an exercise in accepting the present moment, rather than being tense and fearful.

There is only one
of you in all time.

CHARLES BUKOWSKI

Body twist

If you spend most of your time in a seated position,
a twist is an excellent exercise to schedule into
your morning. Lie flat on your back and hug
your knees to your chest. Now allow your legs
to fall to the right, keeping your knees bent
(you could place a cushion under your lower legs,
if you like). Stretch your left arm out to the left
and turn your head towards it. Breathe slowly
and relax into the stretch for two minutes,
allowing your back, side, chest and abdominal
muscles to lengthen. Repeat on the other side.

RITUAL FOR ACCEPTANCE

This ritual is for learning to love and accept our lives, today, in this moment. It is easy to believe that we will be at ease with ourselves at some point in the future, when certain conditions have been met or when we have achieved X, Y or Z – but this means we're always striving for something we don't have and wishing our lives away.

Wherever you are, what can you see? Now close your eyes. What can you feel, hear, smell and taste? Consider each in turn or focus on one of your senses, if you prefer. Open your eyes and look at your hands, at the lines that make your palms, fingers and thumbs unique. Put your hands to your face, and feel your skin, including blemishes, wrinkles and imperfections. This is you. Celebrate your uniqueness.

Let go, if you can, of striving to accomplish – and instead, see if you can embrace experiencing.

LOVING CUDDLE

Whether it's a pet or a human you choose to have a cuddle with, spending a few moments connecting with your dog, cat, child or partner can be a lovely part of your morning routine. Look them in the eye and stroke, tickle or scratch them (if they're a dog, cat or hamster!). They will really appreciate your attention. If it's your child or partner, a gentle embrace for a couple of minutes before you get on with your day will give them a little boost of love to take them through theirs.

MINI DAY-PLAN

Take a few moments to write down three things
you plan to do today – including minor jobs and
activities like booking an appointment or filling a
bird feeder. This is a great way to start the day
with a little focus and to keep yourself on track.
Writing your aims down means you're committing
to them and are more likely to complete them. Even
if your plan is to take it easy, that in itself is a plan!

I HAVE THE COURAGE TO OVERCOME CHALLENGES

PLUGGING IN

This is effective for grounding and plugging yourself into the earth's energy any time you need a boost. You can do it barefoot outdoors if you like, but it also works indoors and with shoes or socks on.

Plant your feet hip-width apart. Imagine you are plugging your feet into an infinite power source. Feel the energy of the universe rising up your legs and travelling around your body, recharging your internal battery and filling you with vitality, *prana* or *qi* (life force or universal energy in Indian and Chinese traditions). Carry this with you for the rest of the day.

Quiet spot

Ten minutes outdoors can be enough to start your day from a calm, centred place. Dress for the weather, go outside and find a spot that feels appealing or draws your interest in some way. It doesn't have to be conventionally beautiful; concrete paving with tiny weeds growing up through the cracks can be just as grounding as a patch of grass, a pond or a tree.

Sit, stand or lie down and allow yourself to slow down. Listen out for sounds – what can you hear? Reach out and touch the area around you – what can you feel?

Focus your gaze on some detail you don't normally take the time to note, and really observe it. Notice any sensations in your body, too. You are resetting your inner operating system and tapping into the wonder that young children exhibit as they experience their environment. Feel gratitude for this wonderful world, and notice how your breathing has deepened, your mind feels calm and time seems to have stretched.

NECK STRETCH

Stretch your neck for two minutes on each side by reaching one hand over your head and gently pulling your head to the same side as the arm. After 30 seconds, look up a little and down a little to engage different muscles. To intensify the stretch, push your head towards the palm and fingers holding it. Release your head and hand, and then stretch your neck again, further this time, if your muscles allow. This is great for releasing tension and freeing up movement in the morning, after sleep.

I THINK WE
SHOULD ALL JUST
CONTINUE TO BE
THE CHANGE THAT
WE WANT TO BE.

MICHAELA COEL

Greet the Day

The time that you take getting ready in the morning can also be used mindfully. Rituals you can do while you prepare for the day include setting intentions, choosing what you will wear, showering, mirror affirmations, creating mental calm and fostering a particular mindset, such as positivity.

MAY I BE WELL IN BODY, MIND AND SPIRIT; MAY I WALK IN PEACE

SETTING
AN INTENTION

Setting an intention every morning is a powerful way to anchor your day with purpose and accountability. Find a comfortable spot in your home or outside. Take a moment to bring your focus inwards, and observe your mood. Contemplate an overall intention for the day – not a list of tasks you wish to complete, but something simpler.

For example, an intention might be something like "I will fully embrace this day" or "I will appreciate all the blessings in my life." It could be a concept, such as "friendship", "fun" or "kindness". Say it out loud if you wish, or you could write it down and display it on a memo board or under a magnet on the fridge. Commit to living this day in the moment when you can, with a spirit of openness and acceptance. Bring your hands together and give thanks for the day, then continue with your morning with a sense of peace and purpose.

TELL ME, WHAT IS IT YOU PLAN TO DO WITH YOUR ONE WILD AND PRECIOUS LIFE?

MARY OLIVER

Fostering positivity

Try meditating on the colour yellow to bring yourself into a positive mental state. You could look at a yellow object, picture or flower, think of a particularly appealing shade, or repeat the word like a mantra. Think of some associations of yellow as a positive, happy colour – a sunny day, a daffodil, a lemon – and see if you can absorb some of that positivity and energy. If you have a yellow crystal, such as citrine, you could hold that in your hand. The colour yellow is also associated with creativity, self-confidence and optimism.

I LOVE, AND I AM LOVED

BRISK STROLL

A brisk, ten-minute walk around your neighbourhood is a great way to get your heart pumping and your metabolism going. You will almost certainly feel better afterwards! Swing your arms and mindfully breathe in the fresh air. Settle into a rhythm and allow your mind to relax into that rhythm, too. Often, our best ideas come when we're in a relaxed mental state, and walking can spark creativity. If you like to count steps, this is a great way to walk 1,000 steps (just over half a kilometre or a third of a mile) before you've even thought about breakfast!

Morning altar

A creative ritual that you may find especially comforting is spending a few minutes each morning making a small arrangement or altar in your home. You can design it to suit the season, the weather or your energy. Begin by noting your mood and the atmosphere of the day. What colours do you feel like showcasing today? Select a few items and arrange them in a way that appeals, on a special spot on a tabletop, shelf or dresser. For example, for an autumnal altar, you might choose to go outside and find a couple of beautiful leaves in shades of bronze, rust or red, and add a rosy apple, orange, nut or cone. You could add a stick of cinnamon and a favourite scented candle, or a crystal in that colour spectrum, such as carnelian or smoky quartz. On another day, you might select a photograph, a hand-written note or a flower as your centrepiece. Sit at your altar and give thanks for all the friends and blessings in your life.

SHOWER RITUAL

Why not make the everyday act of showering into something symbolic and meaningful? As you stand under the water, notice the droplets cascading around your body (and your head, too, if you are washing your hair). Consider the miraculous element of water and how refreshed you feel. Rub a little shower gel between your palms and breathe in the scent. If you're feeling brave, turn the shower to cold and count to 30, if you can. The icy temperature will leave you feeling wide awake, invigorated and ready to embrace the day.

CHOOSING YOUR CLOTHES

What to wear today?! Why not transform this daily decision into an empowering ritual? Consider your mood. For example, are you feeling formal or lively, sombre or bright? Do any particular colours appeal this morning? Picture yourself going about your day. Now look in your wardrobe or drawers. Which items reflect how you wish to express and project yourself today? Select them with gratitude, lay them out and be mindful as you dress. Take time to notice the texture of the different fabrics against your skin as you pull each item on.

MIRROR AFFIRMATIONS

Choose an affirmation each morning to set the tone for the day. Some people stick to one or two trusted ones; other people prefer variety (you could use an affirmations app, if you like). Asking yourself what you most need today to maintain your emotional strength might help you to pick something that resonates. Speak your affirmation clearly, with conviction, to your reflection, and visualize a bubble of loving strength surrounding you.

Example affirmations:

I am here for a reason

I have the wisdom to make the right choices

I will respond, not react

I am letting go of negativity. I am breathing in positivity

I am in control of my own feelings – nobody can make me feel discouraged or unworthy

I radiate love. I value myself and others

I am strong and capable

I look for the beauty in everything

I have the courage to be my best, truest, me

I will make this day count

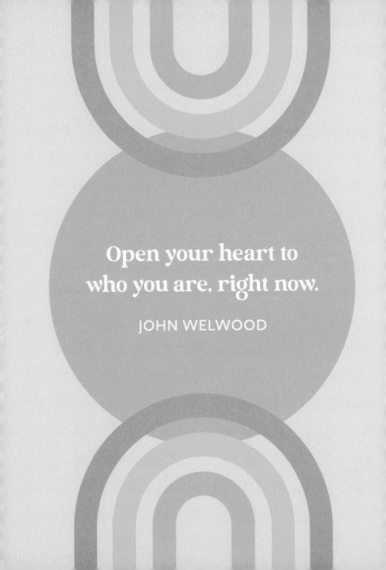

Open your heart to
who you are, right now.

JOHN WELWOOD

LOVING KINDNESS

Commit to living this day with a spirit of
loving kindness, actively looking for the
good in people you meet, rather than
focusing on perceived negatives. Say, "I am
filled with loving kindness," and mean it.
Now go out and practise what you preach!
Beam rays of compassion to everyone you
encounter, giving others a boost – and you
will be surprised at how much better it
makes you feel, too. With practice, you
should be able to extend this to make peace
with those you find especially challenging.

BLOCK OUT ALL THE NEGATIVE ENERGY, AND JUST LOVE.

ARIANA GRANDE

Calming the mind

This is a simple breathing exercise to quell anxiety and calm racing thoughts. It is often called box, or square, breathing. Imagine a soft square and focus on its bottom left corner. Inhale to a count of four and, in your mind's eye, travel up the left edge of the square. Then hold your breath for four, moving from top left to top right. Exhale for four, drawing a mental line from top right to bottom right, then hold for four, travelling back to the bottom left corner. Continue until your breathing has slowed, and your mind and body feel calm.

Daily declutter

A ten-minute declutter every morning is something that can noticeably improve your sense of control. Pick a small, specific area, such as a drawer, a shelf, a corner of a room or a section of your wardrobe. Remove everything and wipe down the area with a cloth. Go through each item and consider: is it something you continue to find useful in your life? If it is, give thanks for it and return it to its place, cleaning it if necessary. If not, decide whether you will pass it on to a friend, donate it to a good cause, sell it, upcycle it or recycle it.

Making this a daily ritual means you gradually get on top of your clutter and are left with the items that add value to your life. It also means you avoid a pile-up of housekeeping that can grow unwieldy and out of control. By choosing to tackle a task daily – with a spirit of mindful awareness and gratitude – it won't snowball into a bigger problem.

FREEWRITING

Freewriting is when people write continuously, without pause, for a set period, allowing the words to flow. It is excellent for facilitating self-expression and unlocking mental blockages. Begin a new journal, devoting it specifically to this ritual. Set a timer for five minutes, and simply write. Write intuitively if you can, letting your stream of consciousness pour out of you and onto the page. Don't worry about spelling, punctuation, grammar or content. This ritual can be surprisingly liberating, as it can alert you to recurring themes or worries you didn't know were subconsciously preoccupying you.

CHOOSING
THE VIEW

This is a simple exercise to remind you that you don't have to focus on every aspect of your day; you can choose the view. Make a circle with your thumb and forefinger, and bring it close to one of your eyes. Look around you: your field of view is pretty wide. Keeping the circle in place, move your hand away from your face and focus your vision on the area inside the shape: it is much smaller and more specific. Move your circle around until you find something that captures your interest. Understand that you can do this mentally any time you like during the day.

THERE ARE
MANY
TREASURES
TO DISCOVER
IN THIS
PRESENT
MOMENT

MORNING PLAYLIST

Compile a playlist of songs that get you
in a happy, energized mood, and play it
when you're getting ready for the day.
You could make more than one playlist,
if you like – for example, a weekend
soundtrack for a lazy Saturday morning,
and an upbeat, lively playlist for busy
days when you need that burst of
encouragement to spur you on. Listen to
your chosen songs, and give thanks for the
music and the energy enriching your life.

SELF-MASSAGE

Giving your poor, hard-working hands and feet a daily massage is a gorgeous gift to yourself, signalling how much you value your body. Pour a little massage oil onto your palm and inhale the blend of fragrances. Beginning with your left foot, work around the sole, heel, arch and top, spending time and care massaging each area. Gently manipulate each toe and the space between them. Repeat for your right foot, as well as both hands. This self-care therapy is an act of generosity to yourself and can help with pain relief, relaxation and emotional regulation.

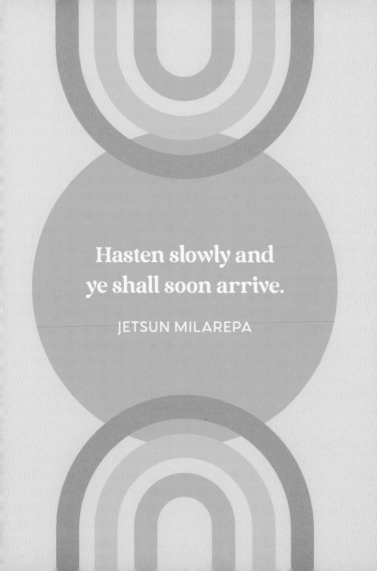

Hasten slowly and
ye shall soon arrive.

JETSUN MILAREPA

Breakfast Rituals

Breakfast is a great time to shift into more mindful habits, preparing and eating your food with more attention and awareness, tending to other living things around you and remembering not to rush. It's even a good time to plan your evening meal, so you can thoughtfully consider ingredients and nutrition.

Mindful tea or coffee

However you prefer to make your coffee or tea, brew your first cup of the day in mindfulness. Turn off distractions and choose your cup. You could wipe your pot and mug with a soft cloth to symbolically purify them, if you like. Make it the way you prefer it, performing each act – such as plunging the cafetière or scooping the tea leaves – with care and attention. Close your eyes, smell the tea or coffee, and think of the journey the plant has travelled to give you this morning gift. Pour it and appreciate the flavour, warmth and lift it gives you.

WE HAVE TO
CARE ABOUT OUR
BODIES AND WHAT
WE PUT IN THEM.

BEYONCÉ

MINDFUL BREAKFAST

The trick to eating more purposefully is to slow down and eat with a spirit of respect. Mindfully prepare a nutritious breakfast, being grateful for each ingredient as you handle it. Take care with your presentation, appreciate the smells and think of the plants or animals it came from, and the sun and water that enabled them to grow. Savour the flavours and notice the textures as you chew. Appreciate the sustenance the food gives you, and eat only what you need. Give thanks for wholesome food that nourishes you – body, mind and soul.

I WILL USE
MY TIME
WISELY;
I WILL
MAKE
THIS DAY
COUNT

BODY SCAN

Breakfast is a great time to do a body scan – perhaps after eating, as your food begins to digest. You might like to start with one foot, scanning up and around your body, and down to the other foot, or you may prefer to start at your head and work down. Focus a few intentional breaths on each area at a time, noticing sensations and any places of tension or emotional stickiness. Mentally, tell any tight areas they're safe and can relax – you could try tensing then releasing, if this helps. Send love and ease around your body, including your facial muscles.

PRESSURE-POINTS RITUAL

This is a helpful daily practice for relieving stress and anxiety. Making a fist with one hand, find the point where your middle fingertip touches your palm. Relax, breathe in and press this point with the thumb of your other hand, and then release as you exhale. Continue for 12 breaths, applying pressure on your inhale and releasing on your exhale, and then repeat for your other hand.

Looking at the back of the first hand you used, find the muscle between your thumb and index finger. Press here as you inhale and release as you exhale, noticing if it feels tender. Continue for 12 breaths on each hand.

Finally, press the point on the inside of your wrist, three finger-widths below the base of your palm, and repeat the process of breathing, pressing and releasing. For all of the pressure points, feel your anxiety lessening. Invite positive energy or *qi* into your soul. Repeat this any time you wish to calm racing thoughts and bring yourself back to the present moment.

BREAKFAST SMOOTHIE

Picking a few fruits and vegetables, and blitzing them into a smoothie is a great way to recharge your body after rest. Choose which fruits and vegetables you want, using a juicer if necessary for fibrous items such as celery. Blend your chosen items with a base of fruit juice or a milk substitute, adding extra goodies like a sprinkling of seeds or a nutrient-rich powder, such as spirulina or matcha. Sip and enjoy the goodness and vitality your smoothie gives you.

DO WHATEVER REJUVENATES YOU... EVERYONE NEEDS TO REFUEL.

JADA PINKETT SMITH

Count your blessings

This is a fun way to encourage an attitude of gratitude throughout your home. Set a timer for 60 seconds (or two minutes, if you prefer) and reel off as many blessings in your life as you can think of, being as specific as possible and keeping count as you go. Counting your blessings is an age-old adage about training yourself to notice all the things to be thankful for, rather than taking things for granted. Do this around the breakfast table with friends or family, connecting and laughing together while remembering to be grateful for even simple, everyday things. All ages can join in – young children, who may need bonus time, might come up with all sorts of things like spaghetti, a dimple or their bunny's floppy ears.

To avoid this becoming repetitive, you could choose a different theme each day or introduce rules, such as only mentioning blessings that begin with the same letter or in alphabetical order. Everyone will benefit from sharing each other's blessings.

I CHOOSE
TO SEE THE
GOOD
IN THE
WORLD

The best way to
cheer yourself up
is to try to cheer
somebody else up.

MARK TWAIN

BE WATER, MY FRIEND

It's all very well beaming positivity and loving kindness around you, but what if you encounter negative energy from others? The martial artist and actor Bruce Lee was struck by the revelation that learning to behave more like water was a useful life lesson. Water flows round an obstacle, rather than allowing the obstacle to block its path. When confronted with a problem, his idea was to respond like fluid and find a way round, rather than reacting in a negative way. Tell yourself, "Be water!" and commit to living this day with openness and fluidity – you may surprise yourself with this flexible, solutions-focused attitude.

Empty your cup

Bruce Lee also wrote about emptying your cup, meaning emptying yourself of your preconceptions and judgements, and approaching a new situation or a new person with open-mindedness. To embrace a little of this wisdom, pick up an imaginary cup and pour the imaginary contents down the sink. Now your cup is empty, so if another person pours tea into it, you will be able to taste their tea rather than sticking to your own. This is a symbolic ritual to remind yourself to greet each day with a willingness to be open to new people, beliefs or experiences. If this resonates, try Shannon Lee's book, *Be Water, My Friend*.

I OPEN
MY
HEART
TO LIFE
AND
LOVE

PLAN TONIGHT'S EVENING MEAL

Taking a few moments to plan your evening meal will pay dividends later. Think about what you feel like cooking tonight, and what type of food appeals to you. Make sure to include a balance of nutrients – you could add a side salad if you need more fresh vegetables. Write this evening's menu on a piece of paper, taking care with presentation, and list the ingredients, checking if you need to buy anything. Now you can look forward to your dinner all day.

FEED A PLANT

You've fed yourself, so now share that nourishment and pick a houseplant or an area of garden to feed and water. Prepare the plant food in water, and pour it over the plant(s) with a smile. Be thankful for the vibrancy this plant gives you, and be glad that you're able to care for it, so it won't dry out and wither. By feeding it, you are helping it to be strong and fight infection. Feel the satisfaction of supporting the needs of another living being.

WHERE THERE'S PEACE, ALLOW IT TO REIGN.

CHIDERA EGGERUE

Good Morning Rituals

Rituals can be done throughout the entirety of your morning – for example, on a commute, while doing a gym workout or outdoors, in nature. Here, you can find rituals to process specific emotions and others to help you find inspiration, forgiveness and clarity.

RITUAL FOR CLARITY

For increased clarity, or any time your head feels foggy, inhaling the scent of rosemary oil can help. You can use an essential oil burner or a diffuser, or apply small drops onto a tissue – just ensure you follow any instructions provided. If you don't have rosemary oil, you could chew a piece of the fresh or dried herb instead, focusing on the flavour that cuts through other tastes. In what areas are you seeking clarity – is it general decision-making, work or a relationship perhaps? Feel your mind clear and allow the answers to come.

I BREATHE
IN THIS
MOMENT
WITH
JOY AND
LOVE

RITUAL
FOR CLEARING
NEGATIVITY

Carrying around resentment, anger or any
other negative emotion is draining. To let
it go, sit for a few moments and embrace
the emotion you're feeling – perhaps
it's a perfectly reasonable response to
something in your life. Instead of pushing
it away, allow yourself to feel the emotion,
even if that's painful in some way. Taking a
piece of paper, write down how you feel, or
key words that you wish to let go. Crumple
up the paper and throw it in the (recycling)
bin. Allow the negative feeling to disappear.

LETTING GO GIVES
US FREEDOM... IF,
IN OUR HEART,
WE STILL CLING
TO ANYTHING –
ANGER, ANXIETY,
OR POSSESSIONS
– WE CANNOT
BE FREE.

THÍCH NHẤT HẠNH

Three big sighs

There is something deeply releasing about a big, vocal sigh. You might feel self-conscious doing this, so you might prefer to do it while alone. Breathe in through your mouth and, as loud as you like, sigh vocally. Do this twice more. With each sigh, imagine you are releasing a river of unwanted tensions you've been holding or any emotional baggage that you've been carrying. Let this river flow out of you, making you feel instantly lighter.

I WILL SHINE MY LIGHT

GOLDEN LIGHT

Hold your palms towards the sun and collect energy – you can do this even if it's cloudy or dark! Imagine golden light pouring in through the centre of your palms, flooding you with joyful serenity. Feel it revitalize your body and soul. If you have any other areas needing healing, hold your palm over the area – for example, your heart – or place it over a friend or a child, sharing your gift of harvesting healing power.

NATURE FIX

People talk of a coffee fix to get through their morning, but a nature fix can be just as effective, with a bounty of bonus benefits! Plenty of studies have shown the multiple positive effects on health and well-being of time spent in nature, reducing the risk of a variety of diseases, boosting mental health and increasing longevity.

Find a peaceful spot in a natural setting that appeals to you in some way. Allow your breathing to slow and notice the sounds around you, such as birds chirruping or the rustle of leaves in the breeze. Reach out and touch something natural – the bark of a tree, perhaps, a clump of moss or a leaf. Let your focus widen and notice all the tiny insects busy with their lives. Embrace a feeling of calmness washing over you, and be grateful for its energizing impact. Notice if time seems to have slowed and, if you can, avoid checking devices.

EMBRACING THE NEW

Every new day brings change, and this ritual helps you to embrace the new. Run a cold tap and let the water flow over your hands. Bending forwards, splash your face and neck, noticing how revitalizing the simple sensation of cold water on your skin can feel. See the water as the new element or change that is entering your life on this one, specific day. Welcome it into your world and give thanks for the newness that is forever unfolding.

A KIND DEED

Developing a habit of doing a kind
deed every morning will send ripples
of joy throughout the universe – and
throughout your own day. You could
decide each time who you are going to
do something thoughtful for, or you could
wait and perform kind acts at random,
for example by giving up your seat on
a bus to a stranger or complimenting
someone at work. Make sure your kind
deed comes from a genuine place, rather
than shoehorning in something artificial.

MESSAGE A FRIEND

Taking a few moments to message a friend or family member to remind them that you care is a beautiful way to brighten their day – and yours, too. Consider what you wish to say. When you bring this person to mind, what is it about them that shines out, and what do they need to hear right now? Make sure your words are sincere and come from the heart. Your friend or family member will appreciate the gesture (especially if it's unexpected), and it is a lovely way to share kindness.

ONCE WE HAVE
HELD OURSELVES
WITH KINDNESS,
WE CAN TOUCH
OTHERS IN A VITAL
AND HEALING WAY.

TARA BRACH

I AM CAPABLE, I AM CALM

Ritual for forgiveness

Emotional freedom means letting any resentment you've been carrying fall away. Allowing bitterness to weigh you down is something you have the power to change, because you can choose to forgive if you wish. Light a candle and think of the person or act you have chosen to forgive. Find a leaf, and write on it the thing you wish to let go. Say aloud that you forgive the person or behaviour, release the leaf outside to be lifted away by the wind and blow out the candle. Let a sense of peace wash over you – and feel lighter.

It begins with
inspiration.

MICHELLE OBAMA

INSPIRING WORDS

Dipping into a favourite poetry collection or book of inspiring quotes can be a lovely daily habit to foster. You could work through your book in order, marking where you are each morning, or you could open the volume at random to see what inspiration or wisdom the pages offer. See this daily habit as a gift from the writers to you, sharing a little humanity across time and space. If you prefer, you can use an app of motivational quotes or poetry and set it to give you a daily prompt.

RITUAL FOR
SELF-ACCEPTANCE

This is an exercise in really looking in the mirror
and seeing deeper than your reflection. Standing
in front of a mirror, gaze directly into your eyes for
a minute or so. Let any criticisms, impressions or
judgements drift away as you focus on the unique
soul that you see looking back at you. Feel compassion
and love for yourself. Now step back and widen
your gaze to take in more of your reflection. Really
look, deeper than the epidermal layers, deeper than
your tissues and organs, to the essence of who
you are. Send kindness and respect to yourself.

RITUAL TO UPLIFT

To uplift your spirits, burn 3–5 drops of lime, lemon, orange, grapefruit or bergamot essential oils, or a mixture of these. As well as being wonderfully nutritious to eat, these citrus fruits share an invigorating scent quality. Lime can be especially joyful, filling your home with a vibrant energy. Breathe in the smell and be instantly transported to a sunny place where these fruits hang abundantly from lush trees – a place where you feel happy and carefree.

RITUAL FOR PROCESSING SADNESS

Sometimes when you're feeling sad, you know exactly what's causing it. On other occasions, you may have no understanding of why you're feeling low. This exercise can help you to process these feelings. Find a smooth stone that fits comfortably in your palm, and feel it warm up in your hand. Tell the stone how you're feeling, and imagine your unhappiness being absorbed into the stone's surface and being locked inside it. Place the stone somewhere meaningful, as a reminder of life's ups and downs, or throw it into a river, lake or ocean if you prefer.

A conversation without words

Rituals don't have to be performed alone. With a friend, sit opposite each other and have a conversation without words. Focus all your attention on your friend and use your skills of non-verbal communication. You might be surprised at how much you can share without relying on words. Conversing without speaking is a powerful way to make a connection and really "hear" another person. It requires more eye contact and empathy, and often a greater level of honesty and candour, too.

I AM FREE
TO BE MY
TRUE SELF

RELEASE AND RENEW

Contemplate who you really are, deep down.
Do you think you are presenting your true self
to the world? What small adjustment could you
make today to get closer to the real you? Breathe
in courage, then let any limiting behaviours,
expectations, judgements, aches or emotions that
are not serving you fall away with your exhale, like
a silk cloak or autumn leaves drifting to the ground.
Let them compost and nourish the earth, and go
back into the universe. You are left with just what
you need for your own inner peace and truth.

GOODWILL RITUAL

Find a comfortable position and allow
the muscles to relax in your shoulders,
face, neck, hands, arms, buttocks and
feet. Be grateful for your body and for all
those muscles that enable you to move.
Allow your breathing to slow. Imagine
you are inhaling a luminous, loving light
and energy. Let it fill your entire being
with its goodness. Give thanks for your
life. Imagine this benevolent light filling
everyone you know, and stretching far
and wide; send it in every direction, and
will it to travel long distances, creating
a tidal wave of goodwill. Carry this
positivity with you all day, if you can.

PEACE IS WHEN THE FLOWERS BLOOM.

AMRITA PRITAM

CONCLUSION

Committing to a few rituals is devoting a few moments of precious time to your wellness. A handful of morning rituals is particularly effective, since they set you up mentally and physically, giving a solid foundation for the day ahead. Deciding to live a more mindful, purposeful morning can only yield positives, hopefully leaving you in a better mental place to handle the inevitable challenges of life.

Of course, avoid packing in too many – you don't want to cram in so many rituals that they become a burden. Instead, make them an uplifting, nourishing part of your day that you look forward to. Remember, you can always return to this book for inspiration as you continue your wellness journey. Most of all, just be present in your morning whenever you can.

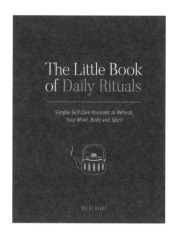

The Little Book of Daily Rituals

Vicki Vrint

Hardback

978-1-78783-224-4

Discover the restorative wonders of daily rituals. With over 80 guided practices to choose from, there is something in this book for every intention. Whether you want to reflect, to recharge your batteries, or rekindle your motivation you will find the perfect ritual to refresh your mind, body and spirit.

Self-Care for Every Day

Hardback

978-1-80007-674-7

Discover the joy of self-care with the help of this beautiful little book. Including self-care inspiration to nourish your mind, body and soul, advice on fitting self-care into a busy schedule, and a raft of soothing quotes, it will help you to nurture your well-being every day.

Have you enjoyed this book? If so, find us on
Facebook at Summersdale Publishers, on
Twitter at @Summersdale and on Instagram
and TikTok at @summersdalebooks and get
in touch. We'd love to hear from you!

www.summersdale.com

Image credit

Flowers © Thomas Pajot/Shutterstock.com